Girl in Cap and Gown

BY HARRIET LEVIN

MAMMOTH books
DuBois, Pennsylvania

First Edition

ISBN: 978-1-59539-029-5

MAMMOTH books
is an imprint of
MAMMOTH press inc.
7 Juniata Street
DuBois, Pennsylvania 15801

www.mammothbooks.org

Cover design & page layout by Jason Enterline

Production by Offset Paperback Manufacturers, Inc.

Girl in Cap and Gown

BY HARRIET LEVIN

MAMMOTH books
DuBois, Pennsylvania

Acknowledgments

Grateful acknowledgment is given to the following publications in which some of these poems first appeared:

Antioch Review: "Property of the Gods"

Confrontation: "Transgression"

Cimarron Review: "In the Community Garden," "Girl in Cap and Gown (under the title, "Then It Happens") "She Ran," "At the End of the Decade of Wishful Thinking"

Connotation Press: "Ibiza" and "Night Walk"

The Iowa Review: "In a Jam"

The Kenyon Review: "Rape Garden," "The Beach Still Dark" (under the title, "Andromeda") and "Key"

Pennsylvania English: "Hemlocks," "Elegy for Kim" and "Enlightenment"

The American Voice: "The Adolescent Saint"

Kestral: "Quaker City Music Festival"

Many Mountains Moving: "Elegy for Ana Mendieta" and "A Lens"

Prairie Schooner: "Boy Soldier" and "King Swat"

Electronic Poetry Review: "Survey of Debris" and "Wrought"

Drunken Boat: "You Walk in Late"

Thanks to the PEW Fellowships in the Arts for the distinction of discipline winner in Poetry and the Vermont Studio Center for a Writer's Grant.

Many thanks are due to Jill Bialosky, Helene Brongniart, Allie Cahill, Tracy Dartone, Sean Thomas Dougherty, Gina Giordano, Bob Grunst, Alice Fulton, Henry Israeli, Jeffrey Ethan Lee, Molly Peacock, Jo Pitkin, Kate Sontag, Michael Waters and Antonio Vallone, generous readers.

for Rick, Teddi and Josh—

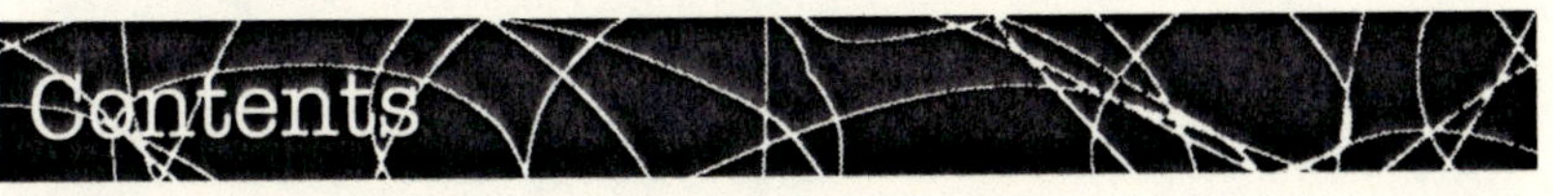

Contents

Part One Girl in Cap and Gown

She Ran 3
Girl in Cap and Gown 4
The Adolescent Saint 6
Elegy for Kim 7
Woman with Bruises 9
At The Threshold of Your Departure 10
Property of the Gods 11
Her Roommate Testifies 12
Mezzo Relievo 13

Part Two A Lens

A Lens 17
Water Being Poured Into a Glass 19
Water Spilling Out of a Glass 20
The Beach Still Dark 21
Hemlocks 22
Rape Garden 23
Clover 24
Enlightenment 25
Quaker City Music Festival 26
Hine Halig God For Ar-stafum Us Onsende 27
Transgression 30
In The Community Garden 31
At the End of the Decade of Wishful Thinking 33

Part Three Survey of Debris

Ibiza 37
Dog Tired 38
Don't Give up On Me 39
Night Walk 40
You Walk in Late 42

Vestigial 44
Bumped 48
Elegy for Ana Mendieta. 50
Boy Soldier 53
Birder 54
King Swat 55
In a Jam 56
Key 57
Overflow. 58
Wrought 59
Survey of Debris 61

But because the parts of space cannot be seen, or distinguished from one another by our senses, therefore in their stead we use sensible measures of them. For from the positions and distances of things from any body considered as immovable, we define all places; and then with respect to such places, we estimate all motions, considering bodies as transferred from some of those places into others. And so, instead of absolute places and motions, we use relative ones; and that without any inconvenience in common affairs; but in philosophical disquisitions, we ought to abstract from our senses, and consider things themselves, distinct from what are only sensible measures of them. For it may be that there is no body really at rest, to which the places and motions of others may be referred.

—Isaac Newton, *Principia*

Girl in Cap and Gown

She Ran

on a path of golden and crimson leaves, everything falling drifting into her. Sweetgum. Ginkgo. Her legs ached, her thighs quivering against the raw weather, breathing in gasps. She ran, her iPod playing Costello, speeding, speeded up, the way light travels, planets spin and meteors collide, leaving a hole in the earth. She ran, her laces slipping out of their knots trying to break free of the soft earth a footprint adheres to, marking her tread. She ran, her hair conferring with wind, blocking her face, shielding her eyes, each turn a wall mixed with some dark and some flashing some brilliant pieces of mica hauled from a pit to shine here. She ran when the path broke onto cement, crossing the blacktop to the other side, stalks of bamboo filtering sunlight. The road is doubtful. The road splits then stops. See, if you rest if you crouch down even for a moment you will lose the energy to find it again, such sharp, such intractable edges. She leapt forward, her sneakers skidding down the curb. In the late afternoon she is not dead, like tree limbs that flicker in the sun besieged with light.

Girl in Cap and Gown

Next morning
over coffee
on the porch of a guest house
in a seaside town, I'm introduced.
Tom says, "You're the girl in the street
last night we called Kim. The one who looks like Kim."
Bob swallows a sip,
then amid the clatter of china, says,
"You could be Kim's sister."

I say I don't know who she is,
and because it is raining outside,
the yellow tarpaulin over the upstairs deck
flapping in the wind,
filling with emptiness,
I go back to my room.
They're still there
when I come down,
sprawled out on the glider.

They scrutinize me, darken my hair,
square off my chin
and I am blotted out. I cannot hear
my own thoughts, voice, story.
The rain and the slap of waves.
The clatter of china. The flapping tarpaulin.
Until at last, I'm off the porch,
having reached the path,
standing in the salvaging downpour
but you have to realize I am writing this
after I have found out.
At the end of that path
I walk smack right into
a pole (literally bumping into it
because it is raining and I walk face down)
where someone stapled a photocopy
onto the gouged out wood

of a girl in cap and gown
splattered with raindrops,
staring at me, that reads:
KIM MISSING LAST SEEN IN WELLEFLEET
6/22/06

I gasp. So this is Kim.
It doesn't matter anymore who she is
or I am or if we resemble one another
or not at all—it had been a pick up line
or at best, a punch,
if Kim were not already dead.

What happens is
they put me in her place
at the bottom of a deep ravine.
I close my eyes. I hold my breath,
the possibility becoming next.
And then it stops,
and I come back.

The Adolescent Saint

1

I'm sorry she didn't press her fingers to his lips and sweeten them.
I'm sorry she didn't lead him out to the fields, dying in autumn,
thistle brushing their bare skin, the world shifting focus until she saw
weeping no more what has always been in this place.
I'm sorry she didn't see the plover coasting in from the sky
to hide in a thicket, its wings trapped, its feathers loosened.
No one reached in. I could not. By the time I learned to cross the marsh
without sinking, the hawk had already clasped the plover in its beak,
dipped in its tongue to drink the blood. What if she had said yes,
circled back, crossed that road, swelled like a milky pod
I rubbed on my bare feet hiking in boots that gouged, scanning the earth
through a lens for black-bellied plover, had walked with him
in the dying autumn out to the fields, would she have lived?

2

Turn the corner and see her shrine, Maria Goretti High School.
R says it was the worst experience of her life, the nuns, the girls,
the catechism: *my body is a vessel, but do not drink from it, do not
press to your lips a single part of it.* She says she's still spacey
as if she were sitting in math class dreaming out the window
incognizant of parallelograms. Would math have saved her?
Would finding the hypotenuse of y have provided an answer
in her father's green fields under crisscrossed grape vines
among birdsong falling through the air, split fruit, scattered seed?
Clad in identical blue uniforms, the girls who go to school here
walk slowly, dragging their book bags. They squint as they emerge
through heavy steel doors then turn to one another to say something
they could not have said inside. I used to talk with my friends about nothing
except boys. We would sit on the bleachers and watch them hurl a football,
fumble at the goal line, bruise us with their attempts at touch.

Elegy for Kim

Hearing's a little flare
the body sends up to corroborate
a stirring. She must have felt
the shiver at the back of her neck,

glanced sideways, then slowly turned
to spot two skinheads
jamming a crowbar into the Chevy's grill.
She reacted to the severity of taunts,

words changing to a quick-freeze
burning the tongue of anyone
quietly repeating them. Archimedean,
she thought she could find the fulcrum

and lever large enough to lift the world,
pushing with all her might.
Even if she did catch herself side view
in the Chevy's mirror, a spasm

of hair flung forward, the sight
was too flashbulb quick and in reverse
to register danger. Would anyone's mind
downshift, contemplate slowly,

as if chess pieces stood in horizontal rows
knights in armor laid out for defense,
or hesitate like an animal about to cross a road,
blinding headlights urging it to go back?

Frayed denim drags across linoleum
and fluorescent lights singe the connection
between knowledge and knowing.
The only facts that adhere

are the ones that fill a can
forced under water
where silt impiously sinks
then rushes clear up the banks.

They grabbed her by her T-shirt.
Did she think no harm would come
to her as long as she was moving,
so out of breath?

Woman with Bruises

Spider builds its web.
Broom imagines edges where debris falls.
House sags at the roof line,
home for a dead sparrow.
Spring feeds a sorrow.
Tree bares itself, cluttering patio.
Arms rise aggressively,
encircle the hour.
Keep breathing.

At the Threshold of
Your Departure

I never saw him take you, never saw you go,
his fingers gripping your arm, the marks
he left, and his voice
vibrating through clenched teeth, winded
and forceful.

The warm bitter piss swill taste of beer
in my mouth, my lips
blistering, as if rigged to a live wire.
The jolt bores
through me,

shock and after shock
with the phosphorescent green
of insects' eyes
or a swarm of fireflies flickering
in bushes

or ambulance sirens whose frequency
I intercept
outside the city's rim.
Ice patches set off
Howitzer explosions.

Black cranium smoke clouds
rise bodiless, for no life can breathe the stench,
rusted and ripped, and seagulls
Bosch-like, shrieking.
It's easier when there are DNA samples,

and strands of hair collected,
(filaments wound helically form cross-connections)
some article like a skirt to stretch flat
and see the actual
linear sequence entwined in thread.

Property of the Gods

There is the blur of color, the yellow
norway maple leaves and the crimson
japanese maples, the firs, pachysandra,
and ivy, twirling and dancing, a wind-
borne dreamland, lightly touching her spine.
The whole time she had closed her eyes,
felt the stem separating from the leaf,
the ripping apart of the tiniest tendon,
which is not a ripping but a mending,
wing and wing, branching, bending
scudding over water. How could he have invaded
her privacy that way? It was narcissistic,
like the way he pours wine, honey to reassure
her. The pressure of his hand on her shoulder.

Her Roommate Testifies

Details, you want details?
Her hair hung forward
all around her face. Her T-shirt
lay crumpled on the carpet streaked with blood.

I tried to ask her what
had happened, but she either pretended
or did not hear me. Soon
there really was too much racket.

With a hammer's cleated hoof,
she ripped out the nails
on her sleep loft.
Using her body for leverage

she split the boards
then stacked them crisscrossed
to ward off whose flesh,
bone and sinew

she was tearing apart.
True, she ran six miles
each morning, but I had no idea
she was stepping onto ground

strewn with such wreckage.
From underneath, the loft had sagged
over me. In its absence
the room looked so large and empty,

as when a reptile sheds its skin
(*take my money! take my ring!*),
stripped of presentiment,
no feeling, no knowledge.

Mezzo Relievo

I touch the crumbling tips
of cattails, the brown powder
as fine as the trail
of sanity Ophelia left
slipping into the water.

Like staying prone, in range,
about to, poised, every view
as through a mirror,
foreshortened, nearness exaggerated.

To come across a thing,
hit rocks, clank, clank, clank,
to squeeze tightly between them
to uncover something glinting,
a back-lit glow, is to
discover the hollows
the dead elusively create.

And then
we are on our knees
digging it out.
In some deep way, the gesture,
though directed at a thing so clear-cut as a shoe,
is proof—in homage to—
the abode, here, handed between us.
And then the recovering
of—as if having begged or wept
over—ourselves.

A Lens

A Lens

It's as if she can't stop seeing existence
through a lens of rape.
Doesn't she have anything
else to write about, things for instance
that if looked at objectively or if refracted
can bend their properties

change states like water, evaporate and dissolve

endure extreme fluctuations in temperature on a faraway planet,
yet retain their elementary bonds

well enough to demonstrate the eviscerating?

Violence doesn't evolve,

its fists and neck-choking hands do not follow the evolutionary chain,
so don't waste beautiful imagery describing monsters
that snap like the short end of the wishbone,

never the half that makes the wish.
They rip through tendons—she ought to write
        about someone who greets with more decorum,
leans over a table, learns to balance water
chestnuts on chopsticks, insulates egg after egg
with layers of Ghirardelli foil to form something distinctive from crown
                             to
                             rump,

bipedal, feathered—something glorious like a phoenix rising above fire
   escapes
and rising over the city, blazing with more light and heat
than the jangle of lights below.

                    She must be doing it
because she wants to be gang banged, fucked like a Yanomami
girl, legs bent so far back

they refract like water in a glass
among the unreflecting panes of glass
in a house, in an entire neighborhood of glass.

Water Being Poured
Into A Glass

I watch you pour water into a glass,
tilt the narrow mouth of the plastic jug
in your unsteady hand. Water rushes
out almost to the brim until you force

it to stop. Glass has a ghostliness
when filled with liquid that's otherwise
submerged. Tasteless, odorless, you can see
your finger through it. You pour that glass

for me to satisfy my thirst. It would
take a flood bearing broken chair backs, tiles
and cornices, crushing plaster walls,

the seepage that destroys foundations.
Yet you persist in confining to
a glass the rippling, churning flow of earth.

Water Spilling
Out of a Glass

Water spills out of a glass as if it always had
given in to anger, shattering its container, its body,
transparent, firm and impermeable. Water drips down the counter

to the floor, splattering more than cabinets, bread box,
ice-maker in the Snow Queen's kitchen. Fury, a small
serpentine river insidious as moisture seeps

through rain forest limina, rotting the insides of things,
termite-infested, flood-lined, destroying the proprietor's urge to collect

objects so rare their worth becomes a paradox:
what the market will bear, what someone will pay when possessed
with the will to own. A sealed envelope flat on a table,

the letter inside folded. Unread. Unfolded,
pummeling on an inter-galactic rooftop thousands of light years away,

the pummeling that when photographed by the Mars Rover,
supports evidence of life. The sweeping of my arm
against an object I didn't see
you bringing me, the unanticipated, out of nowhere flinging.

The Beach Still Dark

The beach still dark,
I run down to the sky,
topsy turvy, vice-versa
mother and father sleeping encoiled
in their ether of unchange.
I am changed. The moment carries me out
like a catamaran, wind in its sails.
It carries me out past teal
to purple bands of water,
reefs sharp enough to skin my flesh,
bony deposits, teeth of the sea.
No, I will not focus on danger.
I will not panic and turn back.
The moment carries me
past wild hyacinth and hills
backing off, silently disowning me.
Wind in its sails, engulfed in bottomlessness,
in fluidity, so clear, so blue,
only as I speak
does it take me away
and as suddenly as I stop,
I am back
under the dull light of stars.
Morning. Father waking enraged,
and mother averting her eyes
so furiously moored
in me.

Hemlocks

These hemlocks swaying
mock the circle of trees
towering my parents' house,
trees that bear no fruit.

No Macintosh. No Russet.
We forfeit nothing by touching them.
I know nothing more
than what I see looking out through rain,

through the steamy window, half-open,
when my mother smiling says,
Imagine the road is the bay.
I don't want to imagine the boardwalk, the sand

the horizon. I want to be there.
These hemlocks separate our house from other
houses, patios, swimming pools, the backs
of parents' heads. Why don't they turn around

and watch us dive into the deepest part
of the water? We emerge shaking,
baring our bodies in the sun.
The hemlocks are a border we can't see beyond

or cross, like the night my father chased us,
when we wouldn't leave our friends, and he tripped
over a branch. In the darkness we laughed,
not one of us rushing to help him inside,

crushing our cigarettes on a curbstone.
Life a succession of images
these hemlocks planted in a row,
green and enduring, we take for the whole.

Rape Garden

Hot and close, half way to death, the splayed branches leak sap.
The trellis sags, redwood shavings trace the residue of the carpenter
   bee's appetite

and the hunger that buzzes, whirls, spins, hisses *honey*
is never satisfied, never at rest. Knowing it will not sting me,

but out of habit afraid, I try to separate
the noise of the bee from its shape, pretending I am traveling inland

and its noise is audible only at the coast, like waves you wouldn't hear
in a quiet little town seventy or eighty miles away,

say, Maldonado, where Darwin collected rocks, plants, and bird
   feathers
and sent them home. In a catalog or museum they tell the story

of evolution, both wonderful and horrible, because it involves survival.
Then I know the sound the bee makes and cannot stop my mind

from zigzagging so that the bee no longer stands apart from what
it touches. I no longer stand apart.

Clover

"Look for the clover in the road," my father says.
From the start, I misunderstand him, a multiple-choice exam,

no fit answer in my head. It is how I construe things.
Wish fulfillment, reseeding itself airborne in tufts.

From his seat, sun-blind, sweating, one leg gone slack
from pushing down on the gas pedal, the rest of his body

gripping the steering wheel,
my father, a tall clipped tree, shouts

that clover is another word for intersection.
And in the face of his anger, I cannot rejoice in the knowledge

that the basest flower is the clover.
Food for cattle. Grown in rotation

with alfalfa and trefoil. A landscaper must
weed it out before it overtakes a lawn,

which, left to itself, it will do.
I slide over as far away from him as I can

to my side, against the door, hoping to open it soon,
as he looks for the clover himself,

in a hurry to get there
without any reason to gather.

Enlightenment

Sometime after mid-term he stops lecturing.
He stands in the center ring of our desks
and stares at us without speaking,
right up to the end of class,
amid the shuffle of notebook paper and backpacks.
I miss the lines of Basho's
he used to recite, the splashing frogs,
flickering cicadas, and ripe persimmons.
I remember thinking, he wants us to confront him,
each of us in our own way.
Is this the full circle of his training?
I do not rest my head on my desk
and dream, but stare back into his face,
listening silently, as if to water,
convinced we are thinking
the same thoughts, that all of us, the entire class,
can hear, in that stillness,
the Voice of Being, of Perpetual Becoming.
My backpack no longer tugs and pulls.
I marvel at the sudden lightness until
almost out the door, I feel a tap
on my shoulder and turn
to face him, breaking his silence.
I become gaunt, moon-white and dream struck
as he puts his hand beneath my blouse,
and, his eyes closed,
he bends to kiss me,
thinking it will enlighten me.

Quaker City Music Festival

The Jefferson Airplane's protégée plucks
            on a twelve-string, the bong's
fired up, passed in anticipation of all
            that's amazing.
We kiss so slowly, our mouths
            nestle inside one another,
echo the sky.
            We lurch up & up & up
through the stratosphere,
            through wisps of clouds
hovering above the voices
            that keep us afloat.
How did I get here?
            How will I get where I'm going?
Mitchello skins an orange,
            but screams that he cannot break free
of his body, cannot
            correspond with Calvin on his decoder ring.
He yearns to comprehend
            the encrypted message.
Someone passes a tequila bottle.
            The worm inside becomes
so close to my mouth,
            so sharply tilted
beneath the breath of music,
            burning and stinging reverberations,
at the bottom,
            bare roots tinged with death.
Quaker City cancels its last act.
            The stadium closes.
We walk the gravel footpath,
            still in it, still swaying.

Hine halig God
For ar-stafum us onsende

—*Beowulf*

In Memoriam, Blake Raphael

Tied to the pickup's fender
the sled glided
forward, then trailed the half
moon's skid.

A boy's screams
claimed shadows,
each in succession
as sycamores stepped out of the darkness,

their joined limbs
seeming to move.
Then he had comforted the boy,
pressed his body against his,

against all that threatened,
darkness, cold, wind,
teaching him to love
the fast ride, the feeling

of motion and of time
speeding up.
Alone with the boy
in the cabin all winter,

the wood creaking
and the fire crackling,
reading him to sleep
from the text

that as he worked on the translation,
clawing open steel-edged consonants
to slip in vowels,
words that grackle in Anglo-Saxon,

thud to the ground,
now hold the hush
of this father's love for this fragile boy.
He came to the part

about the dragon.
The boy's lids dropped shut
then fluttered open,
as he breathed in the cinders,

almost as if Grendel had sprung to life
to never die
and with each relighting,
first roar, sensed stronger.

The strong-hearted
wakeful sleeper
faces the shapes
fire makes, feels only warmth.

He kissed the back
of the boy's neck
before getting up
to throw another log on the fire,

smoothly rolling it
into the flames,
resisting the temptation
to let the fire die out

for the boy's peace of mind.
From his own reading
he knew dragons never existed.
They are composites

of eagles, serpents and leopards
etched in the arboreal brain: wideset eyes,
serpentine scales,
horned hydra.

His footsteps too, touching
down upon
the carpet whose threshold
is now worn, links all other steps

toward and away
the inevitable,
prefigured, then taken.
Painful from the outset,

a retreating world
from such great distance
is a world of slowly spreading shadows.
He pictures the boy

shaking snow from his hair
as if sensing death,
he did not want it
to touch him.

To touch him now
is to feel nothing.
The erasure
as snow melts.

Transgression

You leave with your eggs and toast untouched.
I feed them to the dog, scraps of visible pleasure.
I was a fool to think I could ever close
the precipice between us. You created it,
you, standing taller, higher. All summer
your eruptive mood, your many moods falling
with twilight. I wish you would walk through this door
and see me sitting in this chair, its back
straightened, turned away. My hand doesn't even feel
the plate it picks up, tosses like a frisbee
into the air. That one, then another
and another, as if the crashing rendered
asunder all association and function,
like standing in a hot springs. First we float
separately, the water so much hotter
than our own bodies, it feels like we have broken through
our flesh, sloughed off all color to find pleasure.

In The Community Garden (33ʳᵈ and Powelton Sts.)

Sparse that first spring, we could project growth,
a marking on a cellar wall to tout as comparison.

Healthy roots build resistance like a measles inoculation,
rhizomes, antibody tithers, spathes of the arum lily,

and despite accusations against the use of pesticides.
Native gardens are not special. All flowers belong to the world,

because orchids sealed in plastic on the grocery store shelf
help indigenous growers to compose new songs to stars

rising onto late night stages. You don't have to speak English
to read the applause meter. The peonies amassed with ants
give it rain forest status on the patio of the row home

where I live. According to neighborhood lore,
the Lenni Lenape farmed tracts of ant hills.
Now those ants' ancestors swarm through cement cracks.

The perennials we planted stake out inches of beauty,
spreading leaves overcome asphalt,
stride over the garden's fence, cascade down spires,

blacked-out warehouses and crystalline lots with Sleeping Beauty sleep.
You don't remember waking. You remember ingesting something,
tilting the glass back, then your hand holding the glass grows limp

and it shatters to the ground. If you haven't realized your mistake,
the broken glass tells you. Is it possible that pollen dust,
propagated in spring, mixes with finger print marks

and when the jogger's body is buried underground
she becomes entangled with roots? For example, the myth of Daphne,
her calling out to her father, a god already,

his patience at the boiling point, especially after that charade of hers,
the commotion she caused, the upheaval, disturbing the pinnacle of power.
Apollo at her heels, she snaps back branches trying to trip him,

someone has to throw it back in his face—the privileged assumptions, the
    leaf mold.

At The End of the Decade of Wishful Thinking

In a castle on the Loire,
an American breakfast: hot steaming oatmeal
served in cracked porcelain mugs
that also offer coffee. No Disney rendition of a charmed
Sleeping Beauty waltz between a cup and its saucer
or a cup and bowl. The one mug doubles.

Enough fiber to sustain
a city, stave off the hunger of predators
the way cake won't do.
A staple in the recommended diet for children
who are ADHD, mealtime a chance to reclaim attention.
Sit them down. Focus on the moment.
Whereas touring Versailles

in a motor coach,
having no other distraction
than wind-driven rain; whereas the bronze depictions
of the Rapes of Persephone, Europa, and Daphne,
by Francois Girardon
graphic as they are,
Europa's legs clamped around the backs of a bull's,
are merely decorative, placed in the center of a grove
in the fulcrum, in the fan-shaped striation of the brain;
whereas, today, the sculptor, accustomed to working in abstraction,
might distort the features of the girl and the bull
so that their distinctness constricts,
birds mistaking them for one perch;
whereas a boy who has been fed a good whole grain breakfast
with a week's hiatus from television—

although a week's off is just a starting point—
can be led to see the funicular equipage
of stars. Can look for clusters
beyond the schist of history books
the longer he adjusts his eyes to seeing.

Survey of Debris

Ibiza

I wish I could bumble and buzz,
transfer honey to the tongue
of the stranger gyrating his hips,
his drink in his hand,
and lick off the salt rim
encrusting his tongue stud

with the unsullied swagger
of honeybee daggers in captivity
for three thousand miles
when their crate doors swing open
on almond blossoms.

When I sashay up, he recognizes me
as if after 18 years, an event more momentous
than the honeybee release, because at that moment
someone bumps my elbow
and my drink spills and his drink spills
and as he reaches over
to help assemble
the ghostly broken vessels

his knuckles brush the crotch on my too tight jeans
I'd like to hurridly remove.
Is it just the clinging material
or my soul cleaving
or the solely material
weave of airwaves
collapsing the dark caves
beneath my eyes?

My fingers let go
stinging with ardor
as into the bower of each open flower.

Dog Tired

Just at the absolute moment of heartbreak,
the thud of spirit
lifts me upward
in flying dreams,
soaring in a gust that catches me
in the tipsy swing of its grasp.

Please do not wake me, my T-shirt fluttering,
my hair tousled in air.
All the world's peaks are accessible,
view spilling into view,
pushing open space,
(the blurriness that exhaustion brings)
each red berry within reach,
clusters, in amplitude—

Don't Give Up On Me

Here is a plant its leaves
droop from lack of water or dreams
here on my bed side table.

A shirt sleeve rolled back,
the muscle gone slack,
desperate to stop this guessing

and to know the truth,
the sweat, the one muscle flexed.
I've stayed out all night

and up all night and awake
in the morning racing red lights
to cut you out, and failing that

I've arrived to be greeted by the furniture's
need for rearrangement
in a world of things

that cannot find their place
beset by the demands required
of newsprint columns,

more white space than words,
equally objective coverage to car crashes,
crossfire deaths, floods and bombings

the next days following.
Water redirected from its source
leaks through a pipe,

metamorphosizes into rust-colored residue
corroding the adhesive on the floor tile
buckling at the edges of a swooning universe.

Night Walk

The barking wakes
me after midnight. How he busted out—
the lever on his crate open.

It is as if I myself am called upon
to urinate on roses, shastas, azaleas
but mostly on the espaliers

planted a foot apart
staked up through their hearts
trained to grow straight

in the white moonscape
of the April Nor'easter,
among spewed chunks of ice

and downed branches
where leaves had already died
curled up in wind.

I am called to dig
under it, rupture skin
to reach bone

with stark logic nourished on cold.
Night makes me feel liquidy
cast off in shadows

sliding toward tree limbs,
the locked chambers of tree trunks
that guard enormous rings inside.

As I nose from stick
to stick, the leash pulls me further
away from the house.

Wind haunted trees howl.
My voice a crashing
night voice hurled back

into space like lights
in a skyline
illuminating distance.

And of that distance I know,
feeling my own hands grow cold.
They open the door,

the storm in the heart door,
an automatic release,
a touch of something in the wiring.

You Walk In Late

to class, dressed early instead,
sharp shoulder blades buckled
up through flesh.

To have followed your walk in stiletto heels
from a room overlooking the skeletal view
of an isthmus' oil fields
caged flames, is to hear the fricatives of your native Kwa
crack in our ears as you read: "This is how I am loved."

A choice? You give your grandfather these words:
Not one of my children is here. There is nothing for them.
They sucked the oil until it was dry. Then they abandoned us.
Now like cocks we scratch the ground for a living.

When paws dip into bowls of cream, they leave tracks,
but hands wield instruments: spoons, bellows, shackles, drills.

Your chair scrapes against linoleum,
against the awkward silence.
Your loose-leaf notebook open
on the table, paper bound
in the tightening grip of metal rings,
a grip held equally as tight
as when you string arms against bedposts
and dig spikes into flesh,
as you wait for praise.

Tongue-tied, we also wait
at the corners where you meet men
to use you, slick and rich,
an abundance of crude.

The blackboard seeks to erase
eye shadow on lids,
the flower with cat-o'-nine tails stem delicately
tattooed in the crevice between your breasts,
carried from the Delta. So close
to the heart it blooms,
releasing fragrance into stunned air.

Vestigial

The crisp sound of a stalk being cut with a paring knife,

sound of Seher 's paper,
hardly ingestible truths.

"Look up 'Sati,' barbaric,
the lack of flame retardant material on a sari,"
afraid to write more for fear
she'll release heat in the pods.

The mother who had hunched in close,
suddenly I see her, as if her hissing voice
inflamed my tongue buds,
her eyes well up, her hand
the first part of her to singe,
brushes my hair away,
then rests on my shoulder.
It leaves its mark there, unnoticed on most days
but now makes an impress
the way earth bears the mineral traces
of what our ancestor's ate, fruit and husk,

leaves an impress because of the concentration of the daughter,
the capsicum that opens her airways,
the finally completed escape.
A passage so narrow,
sharp pain
beneath the rib cage,
as pressure to flee
smothering flames closes in.

My eyes sting,
my body's temperature rises.
Vapory steam veils the walls
making their divisions less true.
Soot and ash sifts down,
the pallid stares of people.

Darkness takes me
into its hive where the story can be assembled.
Swelling and burning,
its stingers
puncture my skin,
its antennae scrape my stomach,
its buzzes pierce my ear drums,
its viscosity seeps in through the weave of my clothes,
its organelles duplicate in my memory,
break through my horizon line, my last thing
before sleep, each sip
transferred by mouth
in the glass of water
by my bed side.

What does a daughter do?
She stays out of the kitchen
and away from the stove.

She slips on snow packed steps
rushing for the subway.
She zooms through tunnels,
goes through a dark time
emerges, then goes through it again,
creeping along, heavy enough to muffle thought,
the bitterness of clove,
the pungency of cardamom
and the coarseness of coriander,
traveling away from the dark soul
of the pot, cast iron with baked on drippings
of garlic cloves
with their skins peeled off,
the head no longer intact—

goodness no longer preserved.

Seher describes the boiling point:
her major, Chemical Engineering,
chosen on the Acela Express,
no doubt a pun
connotes a common
misunderstanding.
The catalyst, spark ignited engine exhaust
                         sputtering beneath the wheels,
noticed when she walked,

or more accurately, stumbled through the aisles to the dining car.
Thus activated, her mind sped,

excessively burning up oxygen,

resulting in a net oxidizing condition,

a Siddhartha-like state of attainment of equilibrium.

Remember, she rode on a train, in search of food
she stumbled into the hive
of people, she felt their stares, their stern faces.
Their attaché cases, purses, and back packs
gave the illusion of filled nectar-sacs.
Passing under a tunnel, lights flickered all around,
silhouettes flickered like blue-banded bees as they zigzag
before striking. Then it appeared to her,
the fallibility of structure,
as she passed between the cars.
Metal screeched, as she straddled her feet.
Cold blast of wind, smokey night terrain,
absence of stars, fallibility of weather, planets, systems.
She who lived through the station stops,
doubling and reversing across tracks
in actions handed down, did not combust.

I scoop out the seeds
from a red chili pepper
and mix it with lemon cumin
to correct the spices.

I am lifting my face over her paper—
wandering through fields where steam rises—gripping the handle
of her words. I read:
>*You are numb. You begin as snow begins.*
And then blustery flakes fall—tap at the window.
As children all we want is to be outside
wrapped up in scarves,
anything wool. Snow mother,
inhuman, soft and silent, longed for conversion to cold.

Bumped

On the street where I slip
without recognizing her in day-glo green turtleneck,
hip-hugger jeans, heels, long blond hair,
having just tripped
over the curb and onto a cobblestone
street so skewed
I was almost knocking her down,
sorry even,
after saying so, I turned my head.
To get close to her,
the bag she was carrying and my purse
would have to spill open.

A skepticism, judgments, skewed,
and a spin-off of a complaint,
When I righted myself
who she is to me became less clear.
Leaves shriveled.
Such rules, a contract sealed
when we do not mention what we remember.

It was a way of staying stenciled in,
avoiding the inconsistencies
of the free hand, the torsion
which brings us face to face.
I saw then what happens
when raw feeling becomes refined posturing—that
I turned my head.

I saw how far
her glasses slid. There was now a smeary soot mark
on her cheek. Let's not readjust or wipe away anything,
take advantage of the slight transgression,
see you differently.
The displaced presence enshrined,
you are this now, not that—this.

I understood how the slightest contact
jerks and jolts, how a loose stone
becomes the cusp at which two branches
of a curve greet and join. I walked home
intent on talking with her face to face, the uncertainty
kept me vigilant, with an eye to everything.
A smeary soot mark on her cheek.
The lack of recognition
angered me. Where do I know that from,
her invisibility, her reticence?

It was I who knocked against her,
I who erred, hence apologized.
She turned away. It took me nearly a mile
to reconstruct her figure and turn,
nearly a mile to adjust
the memory like a hemline
to reveal the shape beneath.

Had the blonde hair been bleached?
The curls straightened?
Is the body so mutable to hide its hide,
its hue hewn back?
She got me to search for photos and text,
the stored shot and the injunction of light.
She got me to consider how the frames
fraction off, each one a directive.

I searched the house for my old address book,
many pages frayed.
I have friends who have changed numbers
I gab with regularly,
our voices moving back and forth on a long spiral stretched
to breaking, extensions
of the birth cord. The tone,
the voice, was strange. It was as if
my finger slipped
on the key pad, and my identity
shifted.

Elegy for Ana Mendieta

1

You sit in the shade of the square
drinking Tequila sampled in paper cups
nuns sell in stacked up pyramids
before swigging straight from the bottle
as did every young artist or poet girl
carrying notebooks, crayons, charcoal, Eagle pencils,
camera, mirrors, pages from Aaronson's
History of Painting, in your backpack,
carrying entire decades and movements:

"what can be done, what I must learn,
what there is to do,"
even to slaughter a chicken yourself,
the one clucking in the square,
raising its head to peek
at the dim, shadowy periphery,
before lowering it to peck at dry earth.

All bartering ends with the final price,
the one stripped from our pockets,
the one reserved through the winter months,
stored like nuts in our cheeks,
to be spat finally and to rot,
the price slashed, cut, offered on an installment plan
where the interest piles up.

A crowd piles to watch this haggling
over the price of a simple kitchen knife
used to slice limes to make the hecho in Mexico,
100% agave hand bottled 80 proof
palatable for tourists.

You walk outside town with the squawking
chicken under your arm,
each scratch drawing blood, dug in,
indelible markings of the struggle
to execute one live idea.

You hold the knife to the chicken's throat
and expertly, with one clean strike, cut it,
having breathlessly smeared lines, blurred with an eraser
what is preconceived, yet unknown.

Thus, practiced, you smear the sacrificed chicken's blood
on your thighs and arms,
sweep your hand across your bangs
the way Cortez in the year of the Reed
gets brushed aside and mistaken for Quetzalcoatl
and worshipped as a god
as he openly slashes his way through the jungle.
You lie down on the earth beside an abandoned cistern
as your new husband spreads out the legs
of the tripod, loads the film and focuses the camera.

The photograph is prescient, shadow of your body's newsprint smudge
but back in New York, it can't stop your fall
through the open window,
through the raised, flung open, pane.

2

Maybe I'm leaning out too far
jabbing a corner of the postcard against my fingertip
to stir up the words in the whorls.

Some winds tear us apart.
Others release us
like a figure inside a jack-in-a-box

or twisted loose by the shoulders
like a whelk inside a shell,

connected to the sea that bore us,
dizzy, about to keel over.

Boy Soldier

So hard to balance the picture in this morning's
paper of a Congolese soldier—age twelve—balancing a rifle
across his chest, his innocence in camouflage,

his eyes so bloodshot they portend rivers
risen high above their rims.
Ignominious rains languor and overlap.

The rains take lilies in their clutch.
They take the innate, negligible blossoms.
The photo borders the box where the day's

winning lottery tickets are posted. The glamour
of the winner drives the spinner.
There's no time to consider the dreary font

of a dredge, and I'm unbalanced, grainy,
paying in splits, flicking ashes, and everything else
I look at this sun-soaked, withering October

day is so set on edge, so ready to tip.
The photographer balances the legs of his tripod
over a rut in the road, the whirls on my fingertips as black

as when the psychic held my hand and read
the break in the line, while the next girl dipped
her finger in lip gloss. I'd like to spread her shine,

dab it on in lodes looking for a way to make amends
with others and with myself. A dusky grouse.
A turkey vulture. Even these

lift up. They fly slantwise. They find a vein
to convey them southerly
and go forth astride this tilted earth.

Birder

In the off-hours he reverts
to sparring superheroes,
boomeranging Batman's
lifeless body,

this boy fed on seeds
and crumbs of love.
Now that he's found birds
daylight ignites,

inciting him to
reach, rise, become.
Binoculars raised,
his bird book open,

he wills the ruby-throated
to fly out. Apprentice,
he won't give up
on the idea of thistle

connecting to a bird's cranium,
reincarnating
a bejeweled sky. Through canopies of whirling woods,
whippoorwills, woodpeckers, warblers,

finches, cardinals, swallows stippled
at dusk, delight, stir,
rouse and rescue him in such
abundance, he will not fall.

King Swat

You'll find him in his father's hardware store,
dusty with sun motes, squatting on the warped, creaking floor.
Elvis's plastic bust bemusedly crowds the entry
and radium dials charge the air, infiltrating blood.
Mostly he traps flies under pistachio shells,

convincing customers to bet on the one
that can race the fastest. Transparent angel's wings
burnishing their arcs onto the half shells,
like words etched onto stone tablets,
words of the soul spoken to no one.

He thinks he can save the world,
ex nihilio and the eradication of lawns
flanked with lantern bearers painted in black face.
Illusions of ticker tape parades, medals festooning his neck,
blown kisses and floating petals.

He's King Swat, king of halcyon corners,
king of the buzzless air. Perhaps he can squash the sorrow
that encircles you, the sorrow that lands on your skin.
Sometimes a boy's boastful hand bestows vision,
ever a flick, fine-tuned to the phantasmagoric.

In a Jam

Driving one hour through rush
hour traffic to bring you a spare
set of keys, reminds me of what
I would and would not do
for you. The moon,
weightless lure, stumbles
across the road.
I have been banished
from your sight for lesser sins,
lonely and sorry,
believing lightening would not rift
the same bark twice.
In spring, sap pushes upward
in a body until it flowers
to become nothing more
than wet bark, green buds.
What is the probability
of softening and changing?
The river is a miracle of attentiveness,
eyes and blood, wandering
through a passage so labyrinthine
grief is released,
unlike the place we inhabit
which stands so certain
with a door to lock
and a key to fit inside it.
And if this is the purpose
of all favors, the one requesting
the other to relinquish
that which arms do not yield
then release may,
in good turn, be received.

Key

Arm's yield, body's fit.
        Let guilt not create
                the opening.

            Forced to turn. Stopped short.
Clasped in one hand.
        Vines cut down to reveal
            the dappled on.

        I am waiting.
                Sitting on rattan
                    among the scented,
                focused on emptiness,

      a single notch, a slit,
                    grooved, declivitous,
            sliding into an intensity
                    that is neither unrepeated or
            undiminished.

Overflow

The pond is composed of croaking noises,
noises you don't know you can make
until you give yourself
the freedom—base, guttural. The louder you
become, the more assertive,
amphibian the need. Open your jaw.

Imagine the feeling of saturation, being
bloated and constantly needing more just to
keep level,
a level inflicted upon you. Or is it a
constant
adjustment to excess, going overboard then
dry in mid summer?

Unfiltered, the pond's debris
drifts to the center like prized gifts. Tools made of stone,
sintered vessels crusted with algae buried in the silt,
while from limestone cisterns the rituals that clog history get dredged up.

Ponds that hold the shape of zero get
reconceived as a circle
under the eyes of a Transcendentalist.
Wing and body joined. No fixed reference
point. Grandly genuflecting, one ear
to the ground.

Wrought

Shake what you will,
the hands exert their touch.
Are any birds unnamed,

untamed, left to peck and spill?
Hills dictate hidden
valleys, human sorrow

stored there in earth,
layer and core.
Reaching into a fire

with tongs to extract iron
could demonstrate
how to shape the unyielding,

the anvil greased up
to withstand such thrashes,
the unshaped metal

massive and terrible.
There's a transfer point
where energy's exchanged

but it's invisible,
and we're prone to trespass it.
Salamanders, red-backed,

marbled, spotted
come out at night
to burrow into logs

and feed on leaf litter.
Touch fires the need
for touch. I ask to be handled gently

and mirror my request
upon others. But what do I do
when the will is iron?

Inherent the method
(the Maillart Bridges)
for traversing the steep ravine?

Euclidean blushes
with poise and charm,
sun, moon, stars, torches, and chandeliers,

hang suspended.
No matter by whose two hands
the morning fog is shaped,

it is mine—wind sweeping hair
across your face,
my hand brushing it back.

Survey of Debris

Why wasn't I angry
when the east wind shifted
and everything that was about to be
stopped? That lull intensified,
grew to an uneasiness,
a fraying at the bottom of your jeans
where the denim drags.
Somehow I misunderstood,
took the tension for sport.
My body can buffet me
like a wall against the wind,
against the bleakest of weather.
Can station me in a citadel
garrisoned against the faces
in cliffs and clouds.
Summon the janizaries,
who stalk the ground
upon which we fustian loved.
Mix equal parts of water
and cement to a thick adobe.
Shepherd such a mixed flock.
Contain the threshold
of continuance herewith.